Side Effects

Poems

Lauren Lawrence

ISBN 978-0-9986651-6-0

Published through Shakespeare & Co. with On Demand Books.

for David and Graham

I am grateful to my late friend, Pulitzer Prize winner James Wright, for his generous encouragement during private poetry tutorials in his office at Hunter College, and to the editors of magazines where the following poems were originally published, and especially to Olga Abella, editor of Karamu who nominated "Dorothy" for a Pushcart Prize. Many thanks to my dear friend Michelle-Marie Heinemann for underwriting Ross Leung's invaluable technical help with my Apple computer.

Asheville Poetry Review: "Climbers on Mount Everest," "For the Schoolgirls Who Died in the Chinese Earthquake," "Self Portrait of Francis Bacon," "Preparing for Your Elegy"

Bluestem: "Attraction"

Columbia Review: "Death Raising its Hemline"

Folio: "The Cow"

Kansas Quarterly: "Odysseus"

Karamu: "Articulations," "Dorothy" (Pushcart Prize nomination)

Mississippi Review: "Pomme"

New York Quarterly: "Andy Warhol's White Car Crash Nineteen Times," "At the Metropolitan with Van Gogh"

Poet Lore: "Hands"

Quercus Review: "For the Man Who Died for Ninety Minutes and Saw Heaven"

Redivider: "Walking Home"

Skidrow Penthouse: "The American Infantry at a Time of War," "Almost Motherless"

Texas Quarterly: "Loneliness"

The Harvard Advocate: "On Boat Approaching England from the Hook of Holland"

The Journal: "Looking Back at Twenty"

Tribeca Poetry Review: "Amtrak," "At the End, Dear Mother"

put comma

CONTENTS

When fortune comes along, grab her at the forelock
for I tell you she is bald at the back.

—Leonardo da Vinci

Side Effects

PREPARING FOR YOUR ELEGY

It will be hard to move emptiness—to push its awkward cart

up the dark embankment.

Grief's air is thinnest at the heights.

A lost smile will find another face.

Comfort will tear off its little fur hat and feel the frost.

DEATH'S DIFFICULT HILL

When life's mattress folds like the shy or reclusive, space withdraws—

squanders its mass like something nuclear.

The way spores hit the hard end of cement, I am nothing to grow from.

Let the bracelets of morphine jingle their serious jewels

on your pale wrist,

the slap of your eye sting my skin—and your anger, heavy as bricks

build its guilty monument.

May I bruise in places you no longer touch and soothe.

OBLIGATORY CHRISTMAS CALL HOME

There was the bleak sentiment of a blank page,

words' failure in this deaf, erased moment.

Distant wires cradled the silence, lightened, then bristled.

Hand me the balm that calms hurt's red molecular unrest

when anger kicks in its picket fence and lets the animals out.

Bring back my watch of his infant sleep, crib of lamb, lilies,

harbinger doves, room of no sharp edges.

Something holy whispers this refuge was not forgotten.

The sleeper's arms remain, even now, linked, if not to the flesh,

to the maternal spirit.

SNOWSTORM

When it snowed, it was the clean white talk of heaven we listened to—

the pale souls that shook themselves over the grime.

Some of the windows bore nervous wind, others stood strong,

had variant views—the blink of sun's eye

through clouded minds.

When it was this quiet, things never heard were heard.

The evening snow was a different kind of light,

a transitory joy.

I clasped the congealed snow in my son's small hand

like something to pray over and bring form to the shapeless

unnamed things in this world.

STANCHIONS OF SADNESS

Rain fell, then rusted, Spring's sun unnumbed resolves, but sadness

stood its iron ground.

I slipped on mirage's slicked doorstep; it was what it never was

or hoped to be.

When he left home, he felt holes in the skin, the underlying bones that bore

cerements of the vanquished, and knew to stay away.

Now, like a distant land's coastline, lapped by waves' foam, he accepts the froth

of derelict milk.

Son of blown dreams, spores that never meant to seed in the maternal view,

I know what is missing even though time's gloved thieves

leave no marks on what they take.

DIFFICULT SORROW

There were no words to lay like wreaths on gravestones.

Regret walked back its taut blue coat and popped a button.

Breasts would have traded milk for tears.

When feeling smoked out, I threw bottled water on its desert face,

watched the wretch that was sorrow grow wings, turn angelic,

become unassailable. Who knew?

It takes a long time to be young, but the old always hurry.

COW

It is intended, the imagination whistles after grass, the cow in its grazing fields,

fate's kind pastures of certainty. Wet nurse, suckling the world,

flaunting tradition near a low hedge, the frailty of its hunger confuses

the green stock. Desire has been plucked moist.

The cow shines like a brilliant idea's slow dignity as it kneels, rooted,

contending, by the flowers, where the senses are sluggish

and paused. The imperfect breast, flimsy jowled, delicate mood

of a female, a road made of pure milk. It Is this way, surely,

without pulling, neater than I thought.

*

The cow speaks milk's docile language, appears to be following

some protocol as if future childhoods depend on it.

The past looks backward to understand the struggle of its repetition.

Morning's fingers strain to pull hope from ravines of hosannas.

Nursemaid of the universe, mother's lesson to give of the body its presents.

Suckled nutrient of affection, waiting for the souls

edging into being, mouthing names of the remembered,

rhythms of the internal world's pact of secrecy, until birth

and the cry for milk wired in the mind, authorized, timeless

in the cribbed light.

Around me, night cascades like fountain water

that overlooks its center.

It could be an opening, a dairy place to be milked.

FOR MY SON

When the sun crowned, skylines drew tender nascent shades

like birth privacies. Pigeons ledged at first, tucked their necks in to rest, coo and fool

those who merely walk. At your back, wind relish, ballast, sails, the attraction

of pursuable distances. I poured the sight of you in vats, stored your old games,

left the dim ideas at your feet like Lego pieces, tiny plastic connections

of your old life that need not know it all pulls apart.

Child of no roof, sky wall, light of yesterday's tease,

the pear trees lost white litter.

STROKE

When the tongue froze like winter's lake, she no longer swallowed;

words no longer pointed blame's artic fingers.

Sound stiffened Its grip and girdled speech,

but the beautiful babble continued mother's will toward coherency.

She, in her flower bed sucking on stems that no longer drink.

And I, behind distance's ignorant wall, keyless to open the empty house

with the shades drawn.

ARMADILLO

for my husband

Dressed for war in its serious armored plates,

the armadillo burrows deep, digs shelters where the spirit convalesces.

Its sovereign soul withdraws, learns loss's meaning,

the value inherent in being found.

Resistance is the art of holding back what other minds fill in.

When the claws come out, the tail lowers, the carapace stiffens,

unearths space, the safety of faith's dark aperture.

Behind this mask, the Armadillo grows its placenta's tough skin and retracts,

ball-like, rolling through memory's hallways that any minute now inevitably veer

into kinder aisles of forgetfulness. It must surmount its own bump

in the road, as must you, and commute home.

AT THE METROPOLITAN WITH VAN GOGH

I know you tried to still your nervous flowers' crazed urges;

the disruptive yellow fronds had stepped out of line,

distressing the view.

I heard them choke on your mad roots,

craning their rural heads, muttering necessities.

There was nothing tentative in the arrangement of starch

in your chest—like my husband who fears people.

I am sorry that your soul's bone sticks through the earth

like something partially found.

AT THE END

Nurses said she resisted the sponge baths' last ministrations

of a soiled world. She was no one to play with,

having taken her toys inside like firewood for kindling.

Her hand's tremble shook its brief heresy against youth.

The end of summer worked up its bicycle sweat, rounded

season's tarnished corner and was gone.

There may be root agonies when the leaf leaves the branch.

Will we stay put, you and I? If not by falling, by drying out,

or wearing down like a nub in the fabric.

We share a house with the same windows, the same sky view.

The birds know I have put out crumbs on a ledge.

AMTRAK

My father listened for death's low whistle

deep in the rails, where the crossties and yard switches

urge the body on to different directions.

The dead skim the ground in their frictionless rides. *period*

I blur like fields through mourning's streaked window.

Death's slammed brakes have left me stranded,

in a dark field of the living.

Life is no place to stand still. Even the road lays into itself

for leading me on.

RECOLLECTION

You run through me like a tributary. Let the heavy parts leave

their silt in peace, the shore waves settle into the flatness

of the lost, and sand's time sift and yield.

I crave the late hour when the dark pulls out its chair

and bids us to sit. When the wind flares its skirt,

there is nothing beneath. Where has the past put its things?

DOROTHY

The rutted straw man lacked a brain—he was promised corn,

a deconstructed husk from a stalk.

Words pecked like his worst enemy until he led you to a heartless man

with a silver lining,

a lion holding his tail like a parental hand of deficiency.

The witch's broom bristled, swept its symptoms under the rug.

Courage mounted its resistance, brains grew in cerebral gardens,

hearts banged for acolytes.

If only there were time to interpret the thousand red poppies

you had to sleep with

to cross

to find your way home.

BUILDING RALPH LAUREN'S MANSION ON MADISON AVENUE

Smoke spills from the machines' mouths like gossip at the water cooler.

When there are pulleys and weights involved in the lifting

something enormous hangs in the balance.

Bricks align in a cohesiveness that will stand.

At the end of the day, I am not the only one who depends

on support beams and labors to rise in the world.

GRIEF

When I threw it overboard, the sinking weight

found its hard ground.

Winter's strong bones elbowed through November's wool sweater

and left holes, stairs with no railings,

the wood insistence of a fence where there was none.

Someone asked where you lived and it rained.

HANDS

There was sadness in his hands, anger held in fists' diminutive shelters.

Wrists like desolate willows thirsting for a body of water,

reflection, an upright spine. A finger reached for the steadying hold

of another finger, as if touch were a link greater than any other.

His fists beat, and beat, blocked the entry of the listening.

Then the palm opened as any window, urging the arm

upwards to the light of whom he prays.

ATTRACTION

You were a distraction, the blurry figment

of a loss so bright my eye was drawn there.

Like sky I was shot through with dark birds, turbulence,

Sonar. When you left with the light footsteps of a bride

pursued by a husband long gone, my childish arms

grabbed for the air leaving your body.

PARAMETERS OF LOSS

for Ludovic

Light's lost face no longer echoed in mirrors.

Wind rocked melancholy's trenches, sorrow's lacerations

where reflections were leaving in nervous droves.

There was no ground that would hold you. Doves flew out

when your death cake was cut.

METEOR

When I reach your dim perspective, I may break

in smaller pieces and be lost from view.

I may suffer the sonic boom's bright flashes,

shake the strict walls of your stony space

and move your wind chimes.

You may need to leave the drear behind

in the crater of your depression and recollect my light.

We have lost some of the dance

but there is music left in the tail feathers.

THE COMFORT OF PRETENSE

After you pass, I will look back at you, as I did today,

at the rollick of your knapsack

making its way through the tremble of the haze,

and pretend that you turned around

and met my gaze.

THE WAY OF THINGS

When the body stops wanting, the mind grows its corpse,

hair and nails. The silent caved mouth sets its crater in the field

pursued by different hungers.

It dies the way gloves deflate without hands.

It leans back on the waiting arms of trust, and falls

where bruises go no further.

ANDY WARHOL'S WHITE CAR CRASH NINETEEN TIMES

A car crash viewed nineteen times has no impact.

It becomes familiar—even if the car is upside down and a leg

extends from the windshield like a chrome appendage.

Everything is in place, inevitable as art.

This is how doctors detach and cool the dying,

sever the nerves of feeling.

The surgery runs deep until it never happened.

Until there is no speed left in the wheel.

ALEXANDER

Lined up, stumbling into death, the old fighting,

the mumbled grievance—not much has changed.

When the lowered hand signals battle, blood tightens its reins—

victors are only myths.

When lances hurl, there is no safe place to breathe   *breathe*

in the borrowed armor. The air of glory is thin;

the beggars' cups are full of it.

THROUGH THE SKYLIGHT ROOF

My neck strained on its leash for a bone of attention,

a lap bowl of words.

I caught on your sleeve like a passing mouth's lip stained napkin.

In the evening, when the skylight roof opened, I recognized

the planetary aloofness, the stars' dead lights, as your own.   *no comma*

I slapped my face to feel, but there were other numb places.

POMME

Angling within the aureate fields, the apple swags round and authorized.

A body that burgeons into evening dreamlike, leaves its bright impression

the next day. Morning blazes of apples at anchor in the lower plains.

Eccentric to the trees, a whim elicits water, sunlight, convivial skin—

but the branch never holds the core of its Intention, the waxen

spirit carved, edgeless fruit of an inevitable fall. The clacking mouths

about to measure things out.

ARTICULATIONS

When his words danced, they articulated limbs ~~that~~ *that pulled me in*

~~that pulled me in~~ with intention's strong arms.

When the air grew thin, his voice faded like a mineshafts' lost canary.

Thoughts backed up like bruises draw blood to themselves

without breaking skin.

Nothing surfaced from him. Even silence's abrasive language

was too distant to be heard.

LOOKING BACK AT TWENTY

When meaning lacks weight, the soul steps lightly on the scale,

conveys guile, mirages' promise, jumps with no place to land.

The mind, blurry as a dog's frolic in chewed pillows' feathers.

My braided hair clamored like bell hammers calling the young men.

I was implausible then like something pulled from a hat.

FOR THE SCHOOLGIRLS WHO DIED IN THE CHINESE EARTHQUAKE

The ground let its jaw down and some were swallowed whole.

There is nothing to save those emptied of light.

May they sink in deep enough to come out the other side

and dust the mud off their ribbons.

I have come this far without falling off the rim of my own life.

When the young ones crawl out of their bones

I hope they find a way to the river.

WORDLESS ON THE HUDSON

There were no words that would make the crossing.

Although the wind was fierce there were ruts and runnels in the sail.

The breeze's brine dimmed the light in these waters.

I did not blame the river stars for taking their reflection elsewhere.

The coastguard should have waved me in.

On a night like this even a white gull folds

thin as paper and is gone.

ALMOST MOTHERLESS

Roots loosen where soil has weeded, flowered shambles.

The garden's ground coats like the soot of a war-torn country.

Grief's black shawl swivels its screw into the skin's earth

and cracks its armor.

Even summer blows winter's white smoke,

a smile so empty a bird flies through it.

CLIMBERS ON MOUNT EVEREST

for Sandy Hill

The climbers took their craggy steps and let the mountain pull them.

There were motors in play, but no wheels to turn things around

on this narrow ledge.

I heard their climbing dreams' iron war tools

jabbing at attainment.

But the climb begins at the summit where the elevation peaks

in the thin air of the sun.

FINISHING SEASON

There was less fresh water in the emotional plumbing.

Rivers hardened into land but there were fewer roads for us to walk.

When shards fell from winter's broken window,

I watched where you stepped,

but the spirit weighs nothing on the scales.

You will soon be traceless.

FACE

My fingers traced the features, mounds, depressions—

the rough edges rising inside.

You did not hear me. Your thoughts were a map away

picking apples off a limb, resting your prickly cheek

on the hard, red skin, listening for worms.

LUGE

When fear lays down, the body races, takes the blindsided curves

and finds grace in that reckless bearing.

May I live in a realm that makes you long for my cool descent,

frosted intimacies, bells at the finish line.

FORGETTING MOTHER

From the distance came bricks, a wall formed and draped its window.

When you were so far along, it hurt to look. An arm let go—

climbed the highest rung of the monkey bar and befriended the long view.

Memories shed their boots, exposed the foot, nails, autumnal glare

of the cracked and withered.

DECEMBER BLESSING

The spirit dangles holiday's ornaments

over every giftless thing.

Branches stretch affection's limbs.

Like geese that flee at the sound of a breaking twig,

something quickens, startles in the deep places.

LIFEBOAT

Progress is slow in these waters.

It is easier downstream; a long stroke churns open the fish mouths.

The oars' shift in direction is an abandonment of the past.

If I keep ahead of the wind, the further I am from shore, the louder

the horizon whispers of those that will never come near.

I have lost many faces.

AT THE END, DEAR MOTHER

When it comes, romance it. Insist on the chocolates and flowers,

suffer the wanton rumors of sharing a house, a vast shining acreage

with this new bedfellow.

SUBTLETIES

Death held its breath, the rock-hard pectorals blued.

A darkled shape dug its stairwell until there was no ground left

to fall on but the sky's nurse-white face of hope

of those who go no further.

ODYSSEUS

From the stillness of a room he heard the sea heave,

the serving figures of the waves bring into the anarchy of their bodies

the risen land.

His breath like the blow in a whistle.

SELF PORTRAIT OF FRANCIS BACON

When the self spills like paint from the body into its final shape,

blurs the watercolor edges of this relationship,

runs downstream like rivers that fade in larger rivers,

I will no longer know these brushstrokes as my own.

THE AMERICAN INFANTRY AT A TIME OF WAR

for my uncle

By 1944 the ground troops made an inroad, taking two yards by dawn—

it was this slow. The trees were unusually still.

The first leaf that moves gets it in the head.

The boys marched for months, hawking death on the cheap.

The explosions lie about the pain until they hit you.

Evening's bones glowed like lit windows—like someone was still up inside.

When there was blood on the cedar and the elm, the soul was made serious;

the men looked down at their young hands.

My uncle crawled to the front line at seventeen to battle the Bulge,

shoot his gun, and leave his little trace of ash.

He was the resistance.

ERASURES

When the waves took my footprints with them, I receded,

shore-like, with nothing left to trail.

The dim-witted dark mistook me for a stranger.

In this motherless night, even the light falls down stairs,

bruises, swells with shadow.

SORROW'S PLAYBOOK

Sorrow pulls slowly from the tunnel,

squares its wheels in a nod to resistance,

clings to the old rotation like a forgotten sock in the dryer,

feeds cake to gloom's hunger.

Like grass, it will make its own path.

FOR THE MAN WHO DIED FOR NINETY MINUTES AND SAW HEAVEN

Something about dying opens tunnels of white light.

Familiar faces line the brain shadows' black body bag.

Neurons explode memories' fireworks

at dream's gate, waiting to be let back in

among the wakeful living.

When the mind keys open the body,

when breath bends a candle's light or steams a mirror,

there is always something to climb to get back up.

LAY OF THE LAND

I know the façade of truth when I see something different behind it.

A shattered window is a city divided a hundred sharp ways,

accused by its past, abandoned by its future.

Evening rushes in and bangs its starry head

on the world's roof. Wind scatters seeds of longing in the hopeless

with their farmers' tools, their millet for sun's hoe.

DEATH RAISING ITS HEMLINE

Foreigners, a country sucking blood from its oranges

shades another show, Tito, Tito.

All the promises let go like youths' clammy hands,

the Yugoslav armbands' chilled stripes in the snow.

Nothing mingles for long, you know.

In World War II he wanted to perform, remembered a street but turned

the corner wrong. Xenakis knew the song, the dissonance born

from din's hand grenades before he blew, still as those dressed

for grim parades.

The first tears were rusty from the tap, when sadness strained

from the honeyed sap of nursery years, wouldn't you agree?

The old, languid lap retained more of you than me in mother's skirt folds..

one period not two.

Sun's torn grass, the pale morass limped its way

to the exit door. What was it that the Sparrow saw, sucking crumbs

off the tin guns on the floor? Flying in tandem, no more.

50

CLOSE CALL

It might have happened on my way home when I was ten, and lightning's swift bolt

hit the telephone pole. I was inches from the sky jolt's accusatory finger,

nearly zapped like a bug—marshmallow's black char,

my parents' deep sorrow. But I would have been *the next day's news,*

~~the next day's news,~~ a page torn from a sad book.

WALKING HOME

A fallen petal sticks to my shoe—attests to the adhesive

resin of the dying.

When the small birds feather on I am reminded

there is only air between us.

No cane today, only your voice

leans and leans

against this strange tide that makes its swim for a distant shore.

LONELINESS

Loneliness is added on like an extra wing.

With its low surface temperature, there is wind shear and surges

high inland.

It wets your windows, your floors.

You can slip on it.

Even if you hold on it evades grasp like some vast outer body experience.

It is not a simple thing to kill. Its blueness is made of waters

where there are no ships, against whose mirrors no flashes of daylight distribute.

BOAT APPROACHING ENGLAND, FROM THE HOOK OF HOLLAND

Anxious for the waters to disperse, the land not yet green

and english countryside, buoys were numbering less and less

so we assumed we were almost there. A laggard gull trailed

our map of smoke. It was as memory the lowlands leveled,

collected pieces of time, heather patches, a flower he picked

in Surrey the color of my eyes. The past uplifted,

Britain rose like yeast on the breeze.

MOUNTAIN

When the mountain rose, spirit surmounted rocks like life's little grievances.

In this hushed world, no one spoke of the place where the tree line ends.

When there was no green, the climbers dreamt of rain, seed, sunlight, mother's spoon.

Not the Sherpa's lost blue fingers or the dead's silent climb towards the summit

from which they came.

There are no holes in emptiness—the climber is a hunger

from which nothing escapes.

The mountain is the mind's meticulous ledger of where it has been—

every inch matters.

CARPET

for Andrea Stark

Like the laying on of hands, it smooths splinter's rough edges,

covers the loose planks storing life's hidden things.

It is grass's hushed landscape, rain's shelter

quelling earth's thirst for water.

There are grounds to be covered by something softer.

The way a soul's affect flattens, winter's white blanket

silences footsteps, asks nothing of those who enter or leave.

Within its borders, its clearing, it holds its ground

like a strident idea.

SIDE EFFECTS

Like leaves, I too am something fallen from the branch

among the dark, bruised and dry.

Nothing could restore the loosened grasp, the certainty

of what follows, the chills from within.

The past shuts its eyes when the unconnected strain

for their shadow limb.

Regret drags its broken light to where the land strays

from the familiar.

It was best when the front knew nothing of the back,

the leaves, the rain,

the falling story of the universe at my heels.

BREAKFAST AT TIFFANY'S

We were all stones in God's necklace, cut from dawn, life's unpolished jewel

seizing its purpose to shine.

More than once, I have clasped disappearance's empty casement as my own

and resisted shadows, grew facets that excited hope's radiance, earthen fields

that bid our seedlings' breakfast wheat to stray from its dull chaff

in dreams that begin in dreams.

Endless as light, the voice of the inner jewel speaks the language of rubies, emeralds,

sapphires of the desired.

One does not forget what still remains pressed in coal's dark invective,

diamond's lesson to gleam.

AT THE FRICK MUSEUM

for David

He had those lost Whistler eyes that misplace light in the rarified air

of the rich—

the resistance of the Comte de Montesquiou's cane.

Moving on, Trompe L'oeil was a trick that made me think he touched me

while he stood in Turner's hazy light where it was easy

to tip over and keel.

In the early paintings, it was hard to turn corners without perspective.

I would rather view Fragonard's wall panels and recall my flowering

in the layered luster of permanence,

youth's restored voice, the hoax of mirage's moment, than relive

Lady Duncombe's moment of hesitance. I would rather look from a distance

and believe.

About the Author

Lauren Lawrence is the Dreams Columnist of the New York Daily News, and the former "Political Dreams" columnist of John Kennedy Jr.'s GEORGE magazine. She has published four books, three "Dream Keys" series of books published in 1999 and 2000 by Dell/Random House, and Private Dreams of Public People, a coffee table book published by Assouline in 2002. Lauren is the former star of the A&E TV show "Celebrity Nightmares Decoded" which aired on BIO channel in 2011, and has appeared on numerous TV shows including Dr. Oz, The O'Reilly Factor, Fox and Friends, EXTRA, Inside Edition, Entertainment Tonight, Tyra, Red Eye, RHONY, and other shows. Her many scientific articles on theory have appeared in psychoanalytic journals such as The American Journal of Psychoanalysis, and the Journal of Mind and Behavior. Lauren lives in New York City with her husband.

Books by Lauren Lawrence

PRIVATE DREAMS OF PUBLIC PEOPLE

ISBN 2-84323-339-9 (Assouline hardcover)

"This is the hottest book of the year, a surprising exploratory that adds new depth to dream interpretation. Lauren Lawrence sees humor where Jung saw savagery, a droll thread weaves through her analyses." —Peter Beard

DREAM KEYS FOR THE FUTURE: Unlocking the Secrets of Your Destiny

ISBN 0-440-23479-4 (paperback)

Visit our website at www.randomhouse.com

ISBN- 10: 1-60671-004-4 (hardcover); ISBN- 13: 978-1-60671-004-3 (hardcover)

"Lauren Lawrence's book is extremely valuable. It attempts to uncover the roots of prophesy and unearth what concealed source it grows from." —Pierre Salinger

DREAM KEYS FOR LOVE: Unlocking the Secrets of Your Own Heart

ISBN 0-440-23478-6 (paperback)

"This book is a must-read for the divorcing or unhappily married." —Raoul Felder

Visit our website at www.dellbooks.com

DREAM KEYS: Unlocking the Power of Your Unconscious Mind

ISBN 0-440-23477-8 (paperback)

Visit our website at www.dellbooks.com